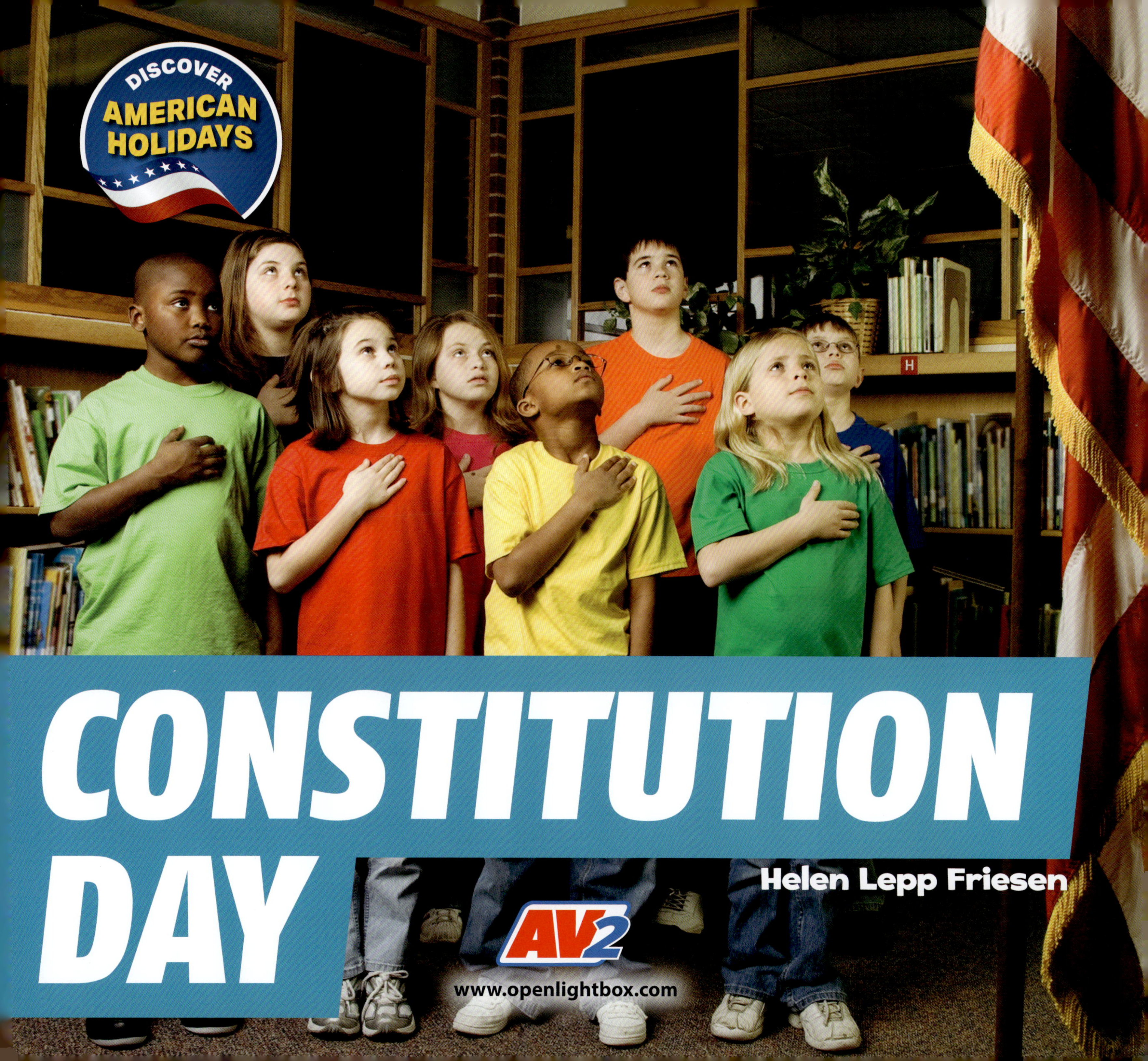

DISCOVER AMERICAN HOLIDAYS

CONSTITUTION DAY

Helen Lepp Friesen

AV2

www.openlightbox.com

AV2

Step 1
Go to **www.openlightbox.com**

Step 2
Enter this unique code
HDAZL76V2

Step 3
Explore your interactive eBook!

AV2 is optimized for use on any device

Your interactive eBook comes with...

Read
Audio
Listen to the entire book read aloud

Videos
Watch informative video clips

Weblinks
Gain additional information for research

Try This!
Complete activities and hands-on experiments

Key Words
Study vocabulary, and complete a matching word activity

Quizzes
Test your knowledge

Slideshows
View images and captions

Share
Share titles within your Learning Management System (LMS) or Library Circulation System

Citation
Create bibliographical references following APA, CMOS, and MLA styles

This title is part of our AV2 digital subscription

1-Year Texas Subscription
ISBN 978-1-5105-8659-8

Access hundreds of AV2 titles with our digital subscription.
Sign up for a FREE trial at **www.openlightbox.com/trial**

The digital components of this book are guaranteed to stay active for at least five years from the date of publication.

CONSTITUTION DAY

DISCOVER AMERICAN HOLIDAYS

CONTENTS

Constitution Day is held on September 17 each year. It is a day to celebrate the signing of the United States Constitution.

The Constitution is the highest law of the United States. It is a set of rules about how the country is run.

The U.S. Constitution became the law on September 17, 1787.

We the People
estic Tranquility provide for the commo
Posterity, do ordain and establish this Con
Article I

8

The Constitution was signed in Philadelphia, Pennsylvania, by 39 men. They included George Washington, James Madison, and Benjamin Franklin.

George Washington was the first president of the United States. He was president from 1789 to 1797.

Constitution Day is celebrated across the United States. Children learn about the Constitution and the rights it gives all Americans.

Some people attend parades on Constitution Day. They may also visit museums or join groups to act out events from the country's past.

Constitution Day is a time to learn. Students read about their rights and responsibilities.

16

Events are held to teach people about the Founding Fathers. These men were part of the first U.S. government.

The Founding Fathers helped unite 13 colonies to form the United States of America.

Today, the Constitution is kept at the National Archives in Washington, DC.

The U.S. Constitution has 4,543 words.

ARCHIVES OF THE UNITED STATES OF AMERICA

Constitution Day is part of Constitution Week. Schools and libraries often have activities all week to teach U.S. history.

Constitution Week is held from September 17 to 23 each year.

CONSTITUTION DAY FACTS

These pages provide more detail about the interesting facts found in the book. They are intended to be used by adults as a learning support to help young readers round out their knowledge of each holiday featured in the *Discover American Holidays* series.

Pages 4–5

Constitution Day is held on September 17 each year. It commemorates the September 17, 1787, signing of the U.S. Constitution. The United States was still a new nation, having achieved independence from Great Britain on July 4, 1776. The Constitution helped the country define itself, its ideals, and the structure of its government.

Pages 6–7

The Constitution is the highest law of the United States. A national constitution defines the basic principles that govern how a country is run. The U.S. Constitution outlines a system of federalism. This means that the federal government shares power with the states. The Constitution also establishes a separation of powers, dividing the government into three branches. These are the executive, legislative, and judicial branches.

Pages 8–9

The Constitution was signed in Philadelphia, Pennsylvania, by 39 men. At the time, the United States had only 13 states. Representatives from each state, except Rhode Island, met at a meeting now known as the Constitutional Convention. The meeting lasted four months and resulted in the creation of the Constitution. Delegates included Founding Fathers George Washington, James Madison, Benjamin Franklin, and Alexander Hamilton.

Pages 10–11

Constitution Day is celebrated across the United States. Children are taught about their rights. Some rights are enshrined in the original Constitution, while others were added over time. The Constitution is a living document, which means that changes can be made to it. Changes to the Constitution are known as amendments.

Pages 12–13

Some people attend parades on Constitution Day. Parade floats are often decorated in the red, white, and blue colors of the U.S. flag. Museums may have special patriotic displays. Some museums partner with historical reenactment groups. These groups wear period costumes and act out key events in U.S. history, such as the Revolutionary War.

Pages 14–15

Constitution Day is a time to learn. Schools and other educational institutions often take the opportunity to teach students civic responsibility. Students study the rights and responsibilities afforded to all U.S. citizens by the Constitution.

Pages 16–17

Events are held to teach people about the Founding Fathers. They were a group of men who helped lead the U.S. War of Independence against Great Britain. They also played an instrumental role in uniting the 13 original colonies to form the United States. The Founding Fathers included the first four U.S. presidents. These were George Washington, John Adams, Thomas Jefferson, and James Madison.

Pages 18–19

Today, the original Constitution is kept at the National Archives in Washington, DC. The National Archives Building also houses the first 10 amendments to the Constitution, collectively known as the Bill of Rights. The Bill of Rights grants all U.S. citizens freedom of speech and religion, among other rights.

Pages 20–21

Constitution Day is part of Constitution Week. The Daughters of the American Revolution (DAR), a non-profit organization, petitioned Congress to recognize Constitution Week. President Dwight D. Eisenhower signed this week into law on August 29, 1956. As a result, Constitution Week is observed from September 17 to 23 each year.

SIGHT WORDS

Research has shown that as much as 65 percent of all written material published in English is made up of 300 words. These 300 words cannot be taught using pictures or learned by sounding them out. They must be recognized by sight. This book contains 53 common sight words to help young readers improve their reading fluency and comprehension. This book also teaches young readers several important content words, such as proper nouns. These words are paired with pictures to aid in learning and improve understanding.

Page	Sight Words First Appearance
4	a, day, each, is, it, of, on, states, the, to, year
6	about, country, how, run, set
9	and, by, first, from, he, in, men, they, was
10	all, Americans, children, gives, learn, rights
13	also, groups, may, or, out, people, some
14	an, read, their, time
17	are, fathers, part, these, were
18	at, has, words
21	have, often, schools

Page	Content Words First Appearance
4	Constitution, Constitution Day, September, signing, United States
6	law, rules
9	Benjamin Franklin, George Washington, James Madison, Pennsylvania, Philadelphia, president
13	events, museums, parades, past
14	responsibilities, students
17	colonies, Founding Fathers, government
18	National Archives, Washington, DC
21	activities, Constitution Week, libraries, history

Published by Lightbox Learning Inc.
276 5th Avenue, Suite 704 #917
New York, NY 10001
Website: www.openlightbox.com

Library of Congress Control Number: 2024939464

ISBN 978-1-5105-8233-0 (hardcover)
ISBN 979-8-8745-1501-0 (softcover)
ISBN 978-1-5105-8234-7 (static multi-user eBook)
ISBN 978-1-5105-8236-1 (interactive multi-user eBook)

Printed in Guangzhou, China
1 2 3 4 5 6 7 8 9 0 28 27 26 25 24

082024
100923

Project Coordinator: Priyanka Das
Designer: Jean Faye Rodriguez

The publisher acknowledges Alamy, Getty Images, and Shutterstock as the primary image suppliers for this title.